Little People, BIG DREAMS®
WILLIAM SHAKESPEARE

Written by
Maria Isabel Sánchez Vegara

Illustrated by
Andrea Stegmaier

Frances Lincoln
Children's Books

Once upon a time, before films or cartoons, there was a boy who enjoyed imagining stories of kings, lovers, ghosts and fairies. His name was William, and he grew up in a busy little town in England called Stratford-upon-Avon.

At school, William spent his days learning an ancient language called Latin and reading old stories. But what he loved most was watching the actors and performers who came to town. That's when his love for the stage truly began.

William was eighteen when he married a woman named Anne. Their first child, Susanna, was born soon after. Two years later came the twins, Hamnet and Judith, just as William's dreams began reaching far beyond his small town.

Hoping to start acting or – even better – writing, William moved to London. He could hardly imagine that he would become a successful actor and be celebrated as the writer of a famous play called *Henry VI*.

Not long after he arrived in the big city, many people began to get sick from a terrible illness called the plague. Theatres closed, and although William had already written several plays, he turned to poetry – using beautiful words and rhymes.

When the theatres opened again, William wrote *Romeo and Juliet*, one of the greatest romances of all time . . .

. . . and *A Midsummer Night's Dream*, a comedy full of fairies, love mix-ups and happy endings. It made people laugh!

But the laughter turned into sadness when one of his children, Hamnet, got sick and passed away. From that day on, William understood the joys and sorrows of life more than ever.
He poured all these feelings into his writing.

Many believe William wrote *Hamlet*, one of his most famous works, while thinking of his son. In this story, a sad prince doesn't know what to do with all the pain in his heart.
He asks a big question about life: 'To be or not to be?'

The story was performed at London's Globe – a big, round theatre with no roof that William had helped build. Everyone, from the noisy fans at the front to the noble guests in the balconies, fell silent during the sad scene.

Then came *Othello*, *King Lear* and *Macbeth* – powerful stories full of big feelings, like jealousy, anger and fear. William's words helped people understand what can happen when we let these emotions grow out of control.

Othello

Whether funny, sad, brave or confused, his characters felt so real that they stuck in people's minds. William used rich rhythms and clever words in his stories. He even made up phrases we still use today, like 'in a pickle' or 'heart of gold'.

When William retired, he moved back to Stratford to live a quiet life. But his stories kept shining in brand-new ways. For hundreds of years, people of all ages have lined up to see plays, films and musicals inspired by his words.

And still today, little William's voice speaks to the heart about love, fear, hope and the big things we all wonder about.

That's why he's remembered as one of the greatest storytellers the world has ever known.

WILLIAM SHAKESPEARE

(Born 1564 – Died c. 1616)

c. 1610

c. 1610

William Shakespeare was born over 450 years ago in Tudor England. Because he lived so long ago, there are lots of things we don't know for certain about his life, including what he looked like! All the portraits you see above are thought to be of Shakespeare, but nobody knows for sure. Shakespeare grew up in a well-off family in Stratford-upon-Avon, where his father was a glove-maker. When he was eighteen he married Anne Hathaway. They soon had a daughter, Susanna, followed in 1585 by twins called Hamnet and Judith. What Shakespeare did over the next seven years is a mystery. But by 1592, he was working in London as an actor and playwright, and was a rising star. In 1592–93, the plague swept through the city, killing more than a tenth of the population. Theatres were forced

1616–1623

1623

to close, but Shakespeare kept busy writing poetry. When they reopened, he joined a new acting company called The Lord Chamberlain's Men. Over the next twenty years, he wrote over thirty brilliant plays and became wealthy and famous. Many of his plays were performed at The Globe, a theatre he helped build in 1599. There were exciting history plays (such as *Julius Caesar*), fun comedies (such as *Much Ado About Nothing*) and powerful tragedies (such as *Hamlet*). All dealt with big ideas and emotions that everyone could relate to, like love, jealousy, betrayal, ambition and grief. In around 1611 Shakespeare returned to live in Stratford-upon-Avon. He died five years later, aged fifty-two. He is remembered as one of the greatest writers of all time.

> Want to find out more about **William Shakespeare?**
> Have a read of this great book:
> *Shakespeare (DK Eyewitness)* by Peter Chrisp
> If you're in London, you can visit The Globe.

Text © 2026 Maria Isabel Sánchez Vegara. Illustrations © 2026 Andrea Stegmaier
Original idea of the series by Maria Isabel Sánchez Vegara, published by Alba Editorial, S.L.U
"Little People, BIG DREAMS" and "Pequeña & Grande" are trademarks of
Alba Editorial S.L.U. and/or Beautifool Couple S.L.
First Published in the UK in 2026 by Frances Lincoln Children's Books, an imprint of The Quarto Group.
1 Triptych Place, London, SE1 9SH, United Kingdom. T 020 7700 6700 www.Quarto.com
EEA Representation, WTS Tax d.o.o., Žanova ulica 3, 4000 Kranj, Slovenia. www.wts-tax.si
All rights reserved.
No part of this publication may be reproduced, stored in a retrieval system, or transmitted, in any form,
or by any means, electrical, mechanical, photocopying, recording or otherwise without the prior written
permission of the publisher or a licence permitting restricted copying.
This book is not authorised, licensed or approved by the estate of William Shakespeare.
Any faults are the publisher's who will be happy to rectify for future printings.
A catalogue record for this book is available from the British Library.
ISBN 978-1-80570-166-8
Set in Futura BT.

Published by Juliet Matthews · Designed by Sasha Moxon, Izzy Bowman and Karissa Santos
Edited by Lucy Menzies and Claire Grace · Editorial management by Izzie Hewitt
Production by Robin Boothroyd
Manufactured in Shanghai , China CC112025
1 3 5 7 9 8 6 4 2

Photographic acknowledgements (pages 28-29, from left to right): 1. The Chandos Portrait, oil on canvas, attributed to John Taylor, c. 1610. 2. The 'Cobbe Portrait', thought to be the only portrait of William Shakespeare painted during his lifetime. (Photo by VCG Wilson/Corbis via Getty Images.) 3. A bust of English playwright William Shakespeare in The Holy Trinity Church, Stratford-upon-Avon, Warwickshire. (Photo by RDImages/Epics/Getty Images.) 4. Portrait of William Shakespeare from the title page of the First Folio of Shakespeare's plays; copper engraving by Martin Droeshout, 1623. One of the earliest portraits of Shakespeare. (Photo by GraphicaArtis/Getty Images.)

Collect the Little People, BIG DREAMS® series:

FRIDA KAHLO	COCO CHANEL	MAYA ANGELOU	AMELIA EARHART	AGATHA CHRISTIE	MARIE CURIE	ROSA PARKS	AUDREY HEPBURN	EMMELINE PANKHURST
ELLA FITZGERALD	ADA LOVELACE	JANE AUSTEN	GEORGIA O'KEEFFE	HARRIET TUBMAN	ANNE FRANK	MOTHER TERESA	JOSEPHINE BAKER	L. M. MONTGOMERY
JANE GOODALL	SIMONE DE BEAUVOIR	MUHAMMAD ALI	STEPHEN HAWKING	MARIA MONTESSORI	VIVIENNE WESTWOOD	MAHATMA GANDHI	DAVID BOWIE	WILMA RUDOLPH
DOLLY PARTON	BRUCE LEE	RUDOLF NUREYEV	ZAHA HADID	MARY SHELLEY	MARTIN LUTHER KING JR.	DAVID ATTENBOROUGH	ASTRID LINDGREN	EVONNE GOOLAGONG
BOB DYLAN	ALAN TURING	BILLIE JEAN KING	GRETA THUNBERG	JESSE OWENS	JEAN-MICHEL BASQUIAT	ARETHA FRANKLIN	CORAZON AQUINO	PELÉ
ERNEST SHACKLETON	STEVE JOBS	AYRTON SENNA	LOUISE BOURGEOIS	ELTON JOHN	JOHN LENNON	PRINCE	CHARLES DARWIN	CAPTAIN TOM MOORE
HANS CHRISTIAN ANDERSEN	STEVIE WONDER	MEGAN RAPINOE	MARY ANNING	MALALA YOUSAFZAI	ANDY WARHOL	RUPAUL	MICHELLE OBAMA	MINDY KALING
IRIS APFEL	ROSALIND FRANKLIN	RUTH BADER GINSBURG	MARILYN MONROE	KAMALA HARRIS	ALBERT EINSTEIN	CHARLES DICKENS	YOKO ONO	MICHAEL JORDAN